BRITISH ARISTOCRACY AND THE HOUSE OF LORDS

Published © 2017 Trieste Publishing Pty Ltd

ISBN 9780649262335

British Aristocracy and the House of Lords by Edward Carpenter

Except for use in any review, the reproduction or utilisation of this work in whole or in part in any form by any electronic, mechanical or other means, now known or hereafter invented, including xerography, photocopying and recording, or in any information storage or retrieval system, is forbidden without the permission of the publisher, Trieste Publishing Pty Ltd, PO Box 1576 Collingwood, Victoria 3066 Australia.

All rights reserved.

Edited by Trieste Publishing Pty Ltd.
Cover © 2017

This book is sold subject to the condition that it shall not, by way of trade or otherwise, be lent, re-sold, hired out, or otherwise circulated without the publishers prior consent in any form or binding or cover other than that in which it is published and without a similar condition including this condition being imposed on the subsequent purchaser.

www.triestepublishing.com

EDWARD CARPENTER

BRITISH ARISTOCRACY AND THE HOUSE OF LORDS

British Aristocracy
and the
House of Lords

By
Edward Carpenter

London
A. C. Fifield, 44 Fleet Street, E.C.
1908

*Reprinted by permission
from "The Albany Review," April,* 1908

WILLIAM BRENDON AND SON, LTD.
PRINTERS, PLYMOUTH

British Aristocracy and the House of Lords

IT has often been said that our victory at Waterloo was a great misfortune to England; and in general terms the truth of this remark can hardly be gainsaid. Our successes as against the armies of the Revolution certainly kept the current of new human forces and ideas associated with that movement at a distance, and warded it off from our shores. The feudal system, broken down and disorganised all over the Continent by Napoleon, preserved its old tradition in these islands. And one consequence has been that, in the matters of our Land-system and our Aristocracy, we are now a hundred years behind the rest of Western Europe.*

Our land-system, with its large estates breeding a servile and poor-spirited population of tenantry and farm labourers, has had the effect

* Not to mention our Penal and Civil Codes, so antiquated and cumbrous compared with the Code Napoléon.

British Aristocracy

of clogging and depressing British agriculture —to such a degree, indeed, that the latter has become a thing despised and neglected by ourselves and derided by our neighbours. And our Aristocracy has developed to so monstrous and importunate a form that, like some huge parasite, it threatens disease and ruin to the organism upon which it has fastened. It is with the latter trouble that I am at this moment concerned.

It is indeed curious that Britain, which has for so long a time boasted herself in the forefront of human progress, should now be saddled with this institution—a reactionary institution of such magnitude and dead weight as no other nation in the world can show. And more curious still is it that, all the time, with great diligence and apparent zeal, she is enlarging and building up the absurd incubus which weighs her to the ground.

Poor Britain! with all her other burdens—her burdens of crying poverty, of huge population, of limited land, of distressing fogs both in the mental and physical atmosphere—to be actually fastening and riveting this extra one upon her own back! What must one think of such a nation? Has she lost her wits, and does she at all divine what she is doing? Is she still lost in a sleep of centuries, and living

And the House of Lords

in dreams of three or four hundred years ago?

There has in the past been a certain glamour and romance about the Feudal Aristocracy. Perhaps distance lends enchantment. We like to lose ourselves in a kind of Tennysonian dream of knights and ladies; we know that once there were bold bad barons, who certainly were a terrible pest to their contemporaries, but whom we rather admire in the far perspective; we do not forget the great historical families, whose largesses and whose crimes were on a splendid scale, whose petty jealousies and quarrels with each other were the ruin of peasants and the devastation of country-sides, but whose *noblesse oblige* had elements of heroism and sacrifice in it, even on account of the very fact of its meaning the maintenance of their own Order as against the world. We may readily concede that these people did some work that had to be done, we may allow that there was a certain poetry and creative power in it; but what has all that to do with the modern Aristocracy?

Of the 550 hereditary peers who to-day constitute the bulk of the House of Lords, it is very doubtful if a single one had a relative present at Runnymede and the signing of the Charter. It is said that only *five* can even

British Aristocracy

trace their families back to that century. In the reign of Elizabeth the lay Lords numbered no more than sixty. Even the Stuarts, who lavished honours on the most dubious favourites, only increased the list of peers by about 100. It was—and the moral is easily drawn—in the reign of George III that the great growth of the modern peerage took place. George himself, anxious to strengthen his weak hand in the Government, insisted on nominating a large contingent—his congeners and equals in point of brains and education—a crass and fat, snuff-taking and port-wine-bibbing crew. William Pitt—and this was part of his settled policy—drowned out the old Whig families in the House of Lords " by pouring into it members of the middle and commercial class, who formed the basis of his political power—small landowners, bankers, merchants, nabobs, army-contractors, lawyers, soldiers, and seamen. It became the stronghold not of blood, but of property, the representative of the great estates and great fortunes which the vast increase of English wealth was building up."* The whole process was a sort of strange counterblast to the French Revolution. But with Pitt's successors it continued to such an extent that

* J. R. Green, *Short History of the English People*, ch. x.

And the House of Lords

actually the total number of peerages created during George the Third's reign was 388 ! *

And from that time forward the same. Britain, to accentuate her victory over Napoleon, and to assure the world of her anti-revolutionary principles, steadily added and added to her tale of titled heads : till now—instead of the feudal chiefs and royal boon-companions and buccaneers and sea-dogs of old days—we have a wonderful breccia of brewers and bankers, colliery owners and Stock Exchange magnates, newspaper proprietors, wine dealers, general manufacturers and industrial directors, among whom the old landlords lie embedded like fossils.† It must be confessed that whatever romance a title may have once carried with it has now quite gone. It is hardly possible, one would think, for the most Philistine Briton or world-foraging Yankee to perceive any glamour in the present aristocracy. Indeed, one may say that—although, of course, it includes some very worthy persons—a certain vulgarity attaches to the class as a whole, and that it is

* May's *Constitutional History*, vol. i. The number of baronets created during the same reign was 494 ! and of knights such a crowd that the order has never recovered from the somewhat aldermanic and provincial flavour it then acquired.

† Since 1800 the new peers created amount to 376 !

British Aristocracy

doubtful whether any really self-respecting commoner would consent to be included in it.

But the curious fact is, as I have said, that it continues to grow and be added to. At present the United Kingdom is blessed with 750 peers in all (not all of them in the House of Lords), besides an innumerable host of lesser dignities. The late Conservative Government, during its ten years of office, scored fifty-seven additions to the House—not a bad count; but Campbell-Bannerman beat all records by creating twenty in the course of his first eighteen months! If the accretions to the ranks of Rank are to continue at similar rates, imagination gasps at the probable situation, say in fifty years.

With regard to this extraordinary freak of "C.-B.'s," it is difficult to find a rational explanation, which—in view of the late debate about the sale of honours to wealthy party supporters—is not also a rather unpleasant one. In the story of "Bel and the Dragon," when Daniel determined to destroy the great Idol which the people worshipped, he fed into its capacious maw fresh lumps of " pitch and fat and hair " (of which ingredients, no doubt, the monster was already composed). He seemed to be nourishing and fattening it, but in reality he destroyed it, by causing it to " burst in

And the House of Lords

sunder." But whether the Liberal party really wishes or thinks to break up the House of Lords in the same way is extremely doubtful. It is certainly an odd way of doing battle.

That it can be for a moment supposed that that House can be converted into a progressive institution by ample creation of Liberal peers is out of the question. In the first place, there is the huge existing Conservative majority there, to be overcome before anything like a balance can be established. In the second place, there is the undeniable and portentous fact that for turning a man into a Tory, a day in that House is better than a thousand (outside). For reasons and in ways not very difficult to see there is a steady social and conventional pressure going on in those surroundings, which gradually transforms well-meaning and progressive folk into rigid obstructives. Of the ninety-two peers (and their successors) created by Liberal Prime Ministers in the last fifty years, only forty-six, that is one half, are now Liberals. Of the twenty peers lately created by Campbell-Bannerman, how many will even call themselves Liberal at the end of another decade? Thirdly, it must be remembered that of those who do thus call themselves Liberals, and under that head are created peers, their real liberality and

British Aristocracy

culture and public spirit (for the most part, and with a few very genuine exceptions) are only skin-deep. They have worked mainly for their own private ends and advancement; they have been successful men in business or in law; they have engineered society influences; they have made themselves grateful to highly placed personages; they have dumped down enormous funds on occasions for election and other purposes; they have even obtained what they wanted by forbearing to press for the payment of debts! In a variety of ways they have been useful to their own side; and sometimes they have been so little useful that for *that* reason it has been thought better to remove them to "another place." But whatever the cause of their advancement, the end to which it leads will in most cases be the same. It is hard to believe—as Mr. Joseph Clayton says in his excellent little book, *The Truth about the Lords*—that the cause of "temperance legislation will be assisted in the Upper House by Lords Burton and Blyth"; or that "the progress of labour legislation, in favour of a shorter working day and the abolition of child-labour, will be hastened by Lords Nunburnholme, Pirrie, Glantawe, and Winterstoke." Having climbed the Liberal ladder, the great probability remains that they will scorn the base degrees by which

And the House of Lords

they did ascend, and retire finally to swell the obstructive influences in the Second Chamber.

Lastly—and most important of all—the probability that the House of Lords can be converted into a progressive institution by the creation of Liberal peers is practically *nil*, for the simple reason that the Liberal party itself is not essentially progressive; and as time goes on gets less and less differentiated in all important respects from the Conservative party —into which in the end it will probably merge.

The whole magnification and bolstering-up of both the House of Lords and the "Aristocracy" generally in this country is certainly an extraordinary phenomenon, and one which would hardly be possible in any other country of the world in this year A.D. Pausing for a moment to take a bird's-eye view of it, and guarding ourselves against undue self-depreciations or too-sweeping comparisons of the Briton with other nations, let us just make a plain matter-of-fact estimate of the situation.

One might suppose that here in the general Aristocracy, among the pick and pink of the nation, endowed with wealth, education, and far-reaching influence, would be found the leaders and pioneers of every great movement; that art and science, sociology and politics would be illuminated and inspired, organised

British Aristocracy

and marshalled by this class; that abroad it would stand as representative of what was best and most vigorous in our people; and that at home and in the country-sides it would set the tone and animate the centres of the most healthy and useful life. What do we actually find? A waste of dullness, commonplaceness and reaction. This Aristocracy does nothing—next to nothing that can be said to be of public utility,* for even the work of the ordinary country gentleman on County Councils and as a member of the Great Unpaid can hardly be placed to its account. It produces (in the present day) no artists, no men of letters of any distinction, no inventors, no great men of science, no serious reformers, hardly even a great general or political leader. And this is certainly astounding when one considers the exceptional opportunities its members have for success and advancement in any of these directions, and the ease with which they can command a hearing and a following.

It is true, of course, that occasionally a man of decided note and ability—a Kelvin or a Tennyson, a Beaconsfield or a Kitchener—on

* It is nowadays enormously connected among the Directors of Joint Stock Companies and Banks and other money-lending concerns, but whether its labours in these connexions are of public utility is a question.

And the House of Lords

account of real or generally admitted service to the nation, and *not* on account of his swollen money-bags or his scheming self-advertisement, is collated into the Aristocracy. But such individuals are not numerous, and they are not the *product* of the Aristocracy. They are importations into it which, alas! do not modify its general character, but too often, like good building materials thrown into a swamp, simply sink into it and disappear. The amount of useful genius or talent which the institution, from its hereditary deeps, supplies to the world is an almost negligible quantity.

Again—not to make too great a demand in the way of world-wide genius or service, but to keep to humbler spheres—we may point out that the class in question does not rise to the occasion of its most obvious duties. Despite the efforts of Lord Carrington to arouse its activity, it does not remodel villages on its estates, or create experimental colonies on its broad acres; it does not meet the very genuine demand now existing for small holdings; it does not even lend farm lands to Boards of Guardians for the use of the unemployed. If these things have to be tackled, they are left to the generosity and philanthropic zeal of wealthy Americans, who come across the water to polish up the old country. It does not

British Aristocracy

exhibit any pride in making its factories or its quarries or its collieries (where its revenues spring from such sources) models of excellent and cleanly management, with the best conditions possible for the workers concerned in them. It organises none of the social reforms in town or country which are so cryingly needed, and which it ought to be so well qualified to initiate. It sometimes *appears* (though, of course, this is not really the fact) as though it could think of nothing more beneficial for its rural demesnes and their populations than to shoot over them, or more appropriate for its town duties than to employ plenty of dressmakers for Society functions.

One must not certainly deny that these good people move up in squadrons, and are greatly in evidence as Patrons and Patronesses of Bazaars, or of Hospitals, or of philanthropic institutions of various kinds. Anything that is colourless and non-committal, which is popularly helpful, without being a severe tax on pecuniary funds or physical energies, and in which a name or a title carries weight, is peculiarly favoured. As Mr. Clayton says (p. 102), "For the laying of foundation-stones, opening of important buildings, presiding over religious and philanthropic meetings, the directing of limited liability companies, the 'governing'

And the House of Lords

of self-governing colonies, and the entertaining of political followers, they are in great demand." And with all these duties, and the demands of "Society" generally, it really would not be fair to call them idle. We may even say that they are enormously busy.

It would be foolish also to deny—what is sufficiently obvious—that among the titled people, especially the older families, there are found some folk of a humane and cultured class of mind, with charming and genuine good manners, simple habits, and a real sense of responsibility and even affection towards those dependent on them; and for the existence of such people, in whatever sphere, we may be grateful, especially in these days when they are in danger of being drowned out by tawdry newcomers.

But all this—in the way of benefits or advantages accruing from the Aristocratic system —is very negative. On the other hand, the positive evils of the system do not admit of being overlooked. To the mass of meaningless fashion and expensive idleness created by our social arrangements generally, it accords an *imprimatur* of distinction and desirability. The flagrant sale of high honours—worse, apparently, in the last dozen years than ever before—corrupts the nation with the resultant lesson

British Aristocracy

that to make a fortune anyhow and to spend it for personal aggrandisement is the best way to gain distinction and public respect. Trafficking in titles has become quite a profession; and a rich man has now little difficulty, through the mediation of diplomatic but impecunious ladies of rank, in getting himself made a knight or a baronet. A quite uncalled-for and disproportionate power is put into the hands of persons who are really not worthy of it, whose aims are vulgar, whose education is poor, on whose tables hardly a book of real merit is to be found (often, certainly, not as good literature as is seen in a better-class workman's home); and among whom the questions most important to be discussed are whether golf or motoring, baccarat or bridge, shall be the order of the day. Gangs of similar folk use their "influence" to get important positions in Army or Navy or official circles filled up by relatives or favourites; and the resultant scandals of incompetence or maladministration, which later years inevitably unfold, are hushed up by the same influences. The nation is heavily injured, but the damage does not recoil on the heads of those most responsible. "Society" twaddle fills the newspapers and impresses the uninitiated and unlearned; the aimless life and ideals silting downwards infect the masses of the people with

And the House of Lords

a most futile and feeble conception of life; and in little matters of dress and etiquette ultimately make the middle classes even worse than those whom they imitate, and from whom they suppose the fashions to originate.

To return to the House of Lords. I have no intention here of dwelling on its record of inefficiency and obstruction. Of its political history during the last century; of its meagre and scanty attendances, even over the most important questions; of its marvellous inefficiency and want of comprehension in dealing with the same; of its indifference when any human or humane interest has been concerned; of its dead obstructiveness when such things seemed to endanger in any degree its "rights of property"; of its clinging to the death-penalty (in 1810) for the stealing of values over 5s., and to the same (in 1820) for values over £10, and to the same again (in 1839) for sheep-stealing; of its maintenance by large majorities of vivisection (1879), and of trap pigeon-shooting (1883); of its turning deaf ears to the pleading cry of children in the coal mines (1842), or of little chimney-sweep urchins in the chimneys (1849), or of evicted and famine-stricken peasants in Ireland (1880-2); of its steady refusal, until fairly forced, to grant the rightful and natural demands of citizens for

British Aristocracy

suffrage and self-government and religious equality and the education of their boys and girls; or to grant the demands of women for rights over their own property and persons, and of men for the protection of their own labour-power;—are not all these things written in the great books of the Chronicles of the last hundred years, as well as in the pages of the Almanacks and the manifestos of Mr. Stead? There is only one opinion about them; and what has been said a thousand times it is needless to repeat.

Nor can we fairly expect anything else. If we indulge in the absurdity and scandal of making men high legislators because they have heaped together huge fortunes by selling "purge" and "kill-devil" to a drink-sodden public, or have made themselves wealthy and notorious by circulating lying and sensation-mongering *canards* among ignorant populations, we must expect the absurdities and scandals and misfortunes which are the logical result. And if it only stopped there! But to go further, and to make the bodily *heirs* of these people our future High Legislators, even to the crack of doom—well, that is surely midsummer madness, and a gilding of the refined gold of folly! As a precise and practical writer has remarked: "Our toleration of this costly absurdity is the

And the House of Lords

wonder of the world. Its like is not to be found in any other civilised nation."

The real question which remains is, What is to be the cure? Dismissing the supposition that a syndicate of American millionaires will buy up the House of Lords complete for the purposes of a world-exhibition, and, on the other hand, the supposition that a violent wave of socialist revolution will drown it suddenly out of existence—as being, both of them, though feasible, beyond the range of immediate politics, we may at least, and as a practical issue, discuss what considerable and radical changes would really bring this institution, and that of the Aristocracy generally, into the line of human usefulness. There is fair reason to suppose that in a few years the Labour party or parties in the Lower House will have a decisive influence there; and in view of that probability some suggestions for a future policy with regard to the Peers may be useful—though the following proposals (it must be understood) are merely individual, and would not perhaps be accepted in block by any of the Socialist organisations.

I think we may assume that, short of a violent catastrophe, the Second Chamber will

British Aristocracy

be retained. Its total abolition would not be in accordance with the temper and tradition of the British; and, personally, I think that—as long as our present general Constitution remains—a Second Chamber is desirable; because our House of Commons—though with an intelligent voting public it might *become* intelligent, and even get to know a little political economy—must always, from the method of its election, be largely composed of professional politicians, and must represent mainly popular ideals, views, and currents of opinion. There is no harm in this, but it requires to be corrected by a more searching, accurate, and experienced spirit (if only, for example, in order that Bills passed by the popular Assembly may be intelligible, and may not become law while still containing hopelessly contradictory clauses). Also a Chamber with some intelligent and public-spirited initiative about it would be very helpful.

A Second Chamber, then, seems to me on the whole advisable, and will, I have no doubt, for a long time to come be demanded by the British people. It will not necessarily be the House of Lords; but here again the British love of tradition and continuity will come in, and will probably insist on its being *called* the House of Lords—even long after it has come to

And the House of Lords

consist mainly of manual workers and advanced women!

The practical question therefore is—how to begin immediately to remodel the Upper House with a view to rendering it (in time) a useful Second Chamber.

The first and immediate need obviously is to drop the hereditary qualification. No son of an existing peer should sit in a future House simply on account of being an eldest son. He may succeed to his father's title (of that more anon), but not therefore to his father's seat. The present House will not be wiped out, but in the twinkling of an eye it will be changed, as far as its legislative functions are concerned, to a body of life-peers. The descendants of the existing peers will (possibly) carry on their ornamental functions in Society, but they will cease to be our hereditary Legislators. This is so very indispensable a reform, and the scandal and absurdity of the present arrangement is so monstrous, that without making this first step practically nothing can be done; and the public must simply choose between this and eternal disgrace. Moreover, it is a reform which could be carried out almost imperceptibly, and with a minimum of friction.

The present House would remain, for the moment, undissolved; but its numbers would

British Aristocracy

slowly dwindle with the decease of its members. All future peers created in order to supply the consequent vacancies would be life-peers. Whatever other titles they might carry, or if they carried no titles at all, in either case their right to sit in the House would not descend to their offspring. Thus in the course of not so very many years we should have a Second Chamber wholly consisting of life-members appointed on their own merits, and neither claiming nor exercising hereditary power.*

What would be the general principles of appointment to such a Chamber ? It might be urged that (after it was once fairly estab-

---

* Lord Hobhouse, in 1894, proposed such a Second Chamber, limited to 200 or 250 life-members, and having also a limited right of veto (*Contemporary Review*, Dec. 1894). Sir Herbert Maxwell proposed that the Crown should cease to grant hereditary titles, and should be content with creating life-peerages ; also that the number of members of the Upper House should be reduced to 268 (*Nineteenth Century*, July 1906). Mr. Frederick Harrison has sketched a similar Senate, drawn widely from the various professions, learned societies, and so forth (*Positivist Review*, Oct. 1906). Constitutionally, the peers are summoned by the Will of the Crown, and apart from that have no hereditary right to sit, and on the other hand it is amply admitted now that the Crown has power to grant peerages and summon peers for life only ; so we see that the change proposed would involve no great technical or constitutional difficulty.

And the House of Lords

lished) it should be made self-elective—say like the Chinese Academy, which for more than a thousand years has exercised so tremendous a sway over the destiny of China. As every one knows, the Chinese Academy consists of some 240 members, the best scholars and *savants* in the empire, to each of whom by immemorial provision is allowed a house and a small salary. The duty of the body is to debate and turn its critical acumen and enlightenment on any or every public question that may arise. It has no direct legislative or executive power; but the results of its debates and its recommendations are widely circulated through the empire, and have an immense influence on the popular mind, while at the same time the body exercises a very outspoken censorship over the acts of officials and even of the Emperor himself. This body is self-elective. When a vacancy occurs the remaining members elect the new one. It is thus independent of patronage, and no doubt (as the remarkable history of the Chinese Academy shows), when once a good tradition is started, this method of election may be very effective.

With regard to the House of Lords, however, there might (at present) be objections to this method!—and we may take it as probable that new (life) peers will continue to be created,

British Aristocracy

and writs of summons issued, on the recommendation of the Premier at the time in office. Assuming this, I think it must follow, as the second absolutely necessary reform, that in all cases a reason (of distinguished service) must be given for each creation. Sir Wilfrid Lawson on one occasion, in 1887 I believe, proposed this. And it is clear that to leave the distribution of high honours and the position of Hereditary National Legislator to the irresponsible appointment of any Government, is simply to court bribery, corruption, and malversation. A distinct and sufficient reason must be given for each creation, just as is done in the case of the award of a medal or decoration, a V.C. or a D.S.O.; and though this in itself might not always secure the best men, it would certainly go a long way to keep out the commonplace and really harmful types, whose real recommendation to-day consists in services which would not bear public scrutiny. Of course this reform will be strenuously resisted by certain classes, just for the very reason that irresponsible patronage is so dear and so very convenient to those who can exercise it; but the change is absolutely necessary and indispensable.

It would probably have to be accompanied by some indication as to the kind of distin-

And the House of Lords

guished service which should be regarded as a qualification. Personally, I think that in this Second Chamber, or House of Life-peers, as far as possible, *every* class or section of the nation should be represented, and represented of course by well-known and well-tried members of such class, or by those who have done good service to their class or to the nation. Lord Rosebery, in 1884, in moving for a Select Committee on the reform of the House of Lords, " specified nine classes which were entirely without representation in that House. The first were the Nonconformists, the last the Workmen. The other seven were as follows—medicine, science, literature, commerce, tenant-farmers, arts, and colonists. He suggested that life-peers should be created, and that the ancient system of assistants, by which judges were called into council, might be revived." [*] Here, at any rate, as far as it went, was a practical suggestion towards making the House an efficient and useful body. But the details of such membership, *ex officio* and other, would of course need careful consideration, and into that question we need not go now. What is clear, at present, is that the future House of Peers (and here the word " peers " comes in

[*] W. T. Stead, *Peers or People : An Appeal to History*, p. 194, 1907.

British Aristocracy

very appropriately) will consist of able men of *all* classes and so-called ranks in society. And this is in the line of a very obvious and natural evolution. In early times the Lords Spiritual, who often outnumbered the Lords Temporal in the House, were not a little jealous of the latter. Towards the close of the eighteenth century the old landed families, who alone beside the Church were there represented, were furiously disgusted at the accession to their ranks of large bodies of commercial and professional gentry. Again, in 1856, there was a storm in the House over the granting of a life-peerage to Lord Wensleydale; the highest legal and historical authorities, however, maintained that it was the ancient right and privilege of the Crown to create life-peers; and in 1887 the Appellate Jurisdiction Act was passed, in accordance with which certain Law-lords now take their seats for life *ex officio*. Finally, in the last twenty years, classes of men have been admitted to the House whom even George III would not have dared to propose. Sir Erskine May, in his *Constitutional History of England*, speaking of the great growth in numbers of the Upper House in modern times, says: " With this large increase of numbers the peerage has undergone further changes no less remarkable, in its character and composition. It is no

And the House of Lords

longer a council of the magnates of the Land—the territorial Aristocracy, the descendants or representatives of the barons of the olden time; but in each successive age it has assumed a more popular and representative character." Thus, although the present House would, no doubt, be much shocked at the idea, it does not seem at all improbable that a time may come when a Joseph Arch, for instance, as an eminent farm-labourer and representative of farm-labourers, might be called to sit on its councils.

Another reform which will probably be advisable will be the limitation of the new House of Life-peers to a definite number of members—although, of course, such limiting number might be alterable from time to time. One great advantage of such a limitation is, that on any occasion the number of vacancies existing is known, and the question of their replenishment comes naturally before the public, so that, whoever the appointing authority may be, he or they cannot easily act in a secret or underhand way in the matter, as is indeed too possible with the present method.

The reforms thus proposed are practically three :—

1. Life-peerages (the actual title a matter of little importance).

British Aristocracy

2. Adequate reasons of useful service to be given for each creation—on democratic grounds more or less scheduled and recognised.

3. Limitation of number of members.

Under such conditions as these reforms would induce, the Second Chamber would probably turn out satisfactorily, and there does not seem any reasons why its powers should be seriously curtailed. To propose to keep the House of Lords as it is, is practically to *ask* for the curtailment of its powers and the suspension of the right of veto—for it is evident that things cannot go on very long as they are; but to remove the right of veto would in effect be to reduce the House to a mere revising body—whose work could, of course, be better done by a committee of experts. If a Second Chamber is to be retained at all, far more sensible would it be to make it a really useful and intelligent institution, with power of initiative and power of veto—the latter at any rate to some degree, though of course guarded. Short of our securing such useful and intelligent body, Abolition would be the only alternative.

There remain a few words to say about the Aristocracy generally, and the possibilities of bringing it into line as a serviceable or even

And the House of Lords

tolerable institution. It is fairly clear that the same arguments which have been brought forward in favour of a life-seat only in the House of Peers, and in favour of a declaration of the reasons for conferring that distinction, apply equally—though not perhaps equally pressingly—to the conferring of titles generally. Of course, it would be possible to raise a man to a baronage or an earldom, and in doing so to give him a life-seat only in the Second Chamber, while at the same time continuing his *title* to his heirs; but the question arises, Why—because a man has done useful service to the nation (assuming, of course, that he has), and the nation to show its gratitude confers some title upon him—why should the irresponsible heirs of this man, and of other such men, be allowed *in perpetuo* to sport similar titles, and so to form (as we see) a class of Society idlers (or busybodies) who, to say the least, exercise an enfeebling and unworthy influence on the rest of the people?* It may be replied to that, that as long as you take from such folk direct legislative power, the thing does

---

* It should also be pointed out that if it is desired to confer distinction by titles, the latter *must* be for life only —since the hereditary system gives no distinction, no distinction between authentic genius and the commonplace wearer of a family coronet.

British Aristocracy

not matter. If any such classes like to whirl round in their little coteries, and have their smart dinner-parties and their scandals, their punctilios of precedence and their privileges of heading lists of subscriptions, why should the nation interfere to deprive them of these simple pleasures? And there is so far truth in this, that we must admit that as long as the present commercial system continues, and there remains, as to-day, a sum of some 600 millions sterling of *unearned* income, or more, to be divided every year among the capitalist and landlord classes, this feeble and unworthy life *will* probably continue among such classes, whether titled or not. That is so far true; but it forms no reason why the nation, by a system of rank without service, should give its *imprimatur* of distinction to such a life.

Again, there may be some people who believe in Blood so far as to think that the descendants of a really great man inherit his virtues to a remote posterity. And it certainly seems possible that some day—when there is a State department of Eugenics—whole families may be granted a pedigree and diploma on account of their excellent breed; but then I need hardly say that such patent of nobility would be immediately cancelled for any person who should breed children outside the regula-

And the House of Lords

tion of the State—as I fear many of our aristocracy at present do! And as to the Blood descending *with the Name*, a very brief calculation will dispel that illusion, for it is easily found (doubling at each generation) that *ten* generations back one had over a thousand ancestors living (say in 1600 A.D.), while ten generations again before that (say in 1300) one had over a *million*. Any one, therefore, who can trace his descent from some ancestor living in 1300—and there are few indeed who can do that—will have the satisfaction of knowing that one-millionth * part of the blood in his veins will be due to that ancestor!

I have referred—in speaking of the House of Lords—to the Chinese Academy, which seems an extraordinarily practical and sensible institution. We might do worse than take a hint from China as to the handling of titles generally. Greatly and devoutly as John Chinaman believes in heredity, descent, and ancestor-worship, he is not such a fool as to close his eyes to the fact that blood very soon runs out and becomes intermixed. Chester Holcombe,

---

* It is true that, according to the Mendelian theory of heredity, there may occasionally emerge a very near replica of some fairly remote ancestor; but, as I say, it will in all probability be of an ancestor *not* in the line of the Name.

British Aristocracy

for some years Acting Minister of the United States at Pekin, says of the Chinese in his excellent book, *The Real Chinaman*: "There is no titled nobility, with its long list of elder and younger sons, sons-in-law, and cousins near and remote, to be supported from the public funds, and to fill all the more important positions of honour and profit. The few titles that are from time to time bestowed carry nothing with them but the nominal honour; they are bestowed as rewards for distinguished services, and have never been recognised as forming the basis of any claim whatever upon either offices or treasury. In a way they are hereditary, but soon run out, *since the rank decreases one grade with each generation*. Even the imperial clan forms no exception to this rule. The author has many a time had in his employ a man who, as a relative of the Emperor, was entitled to wear the imperial yellow girdle; but he was a hod-carrier, and earned six cents a day."

With this suggestion—for the benefit of some future Government—I will close. Let our Aristocracy, as far as it is hereditary, be "let down gently" by the rank descending one grade with each generation. This already happens with the younger children of our higher ranks,

And the House of Lords

who receive courtesy titles for life. Let a system of such courtesy titles be extended for two or three generations, and let all children in that respect count as younger children; and in a few years we should have got rid of a foolish and somewhat vulgar anachronism.

THE END

Works by Edward Carpenter

(Published by SWAN SONNENSCHEIN & Co. LTD. Those marked *
published also by S. CLARKE, Manchester.)

*TOWARDS DEMOCRACY: Complete Poems in four parts. Library Edition, one vol., crown 8vo, pp. 506, cloth gilt. 3/6 nett.

*The same. Pocket Edition, one vol., India paper, limp binding, gilt edge. 3/6 nett.

WHO SHALL COMMAND THE HEART. Being Part IV of TOWARDS DEMOCRACY. One vol., pp. 150, cloth, gilt edge. 2/- nett.

ENGLAND'S IDEAL, and other Papers on Social Subjects. Fourth Edition, 1902, pp. 176. Cloth, 2/6; paper, 1/-

CIVILISATION: ITS CAUSE AND CURE. Essays on Modern Science, &c. Ninth Edition, 1906, pp. 176. Cloth, 2/6; paper, 1/-

*LOVE'S COMING OF AGE: a Series of Papers on the Relations of the Sexes. Fifth Edition, 1906, pp. 190. Cloth, 3/6 nett.

ANGELS' WINGS: Essays on Art and Life, with nine full-page plates, cloth gilt, pp. 248. 4/6 nett.

ADAM'S PEAK TO ELEPHANTA: Sketches in Ceylon and India. New Edition, 1903. Cloth gilt, 4/6.

THE STORY OF EROS AND PSYCHE, with first book of Homer's Iliad done into English, and frontispiece. Cloth gilt, 2/6.

*IOLÄUS: An Anthology of Friendship. Printed in Old Face Caslon type, with ornamental initials and side notes. New and Enlarged Edition. Cloth, gilt edge, 2/6 nett.

Works by Edward Carpenter *(continued)*:

CHANTS OF LABOUR: A Song-book for the People, edited by EDWARD CARPENTER. With frontispiece and cover by WALTER CRANE. Paper, 1/-.

(Published by GEORGE ALLEN.)

THE ART OF CREATION: Essays on the Self and its Powers. Second Edition, enlarged, 1907. Crown 8vo, cloth gilt, pp. 266. 5/- nett.

DAYS WITH WALT WHITMAN, with some Notes on his Life and Work, and three portraits. Crown 8vo, cloth gilt. 5/- nett. 1906.

SKETCHES FROM LIFE IN TOWN AND COUNTRY, with some verses. 1908. 5/- nett.

(Published by A. C. FIFIELD, 44 Fleet Street, E.C.)

PRISONS, POLICE, AND PUNISHMENT: An Inquiry into the Causes and Treatment of Crime and Criminals. Crown 8vo, cloth, 2/- nett. 1905. Paper, 1/- nett.

VIVISECTION: Two Addresses. New Edition. Price 3d. nett.

EMPIRE IN INDIA AND ELSEWHERE. Pamphlet. New Edition. Price 2d.

HUMANE SCIENCE. Pamphlet. 2d.

BRITISH ARISTOCRACY AND THE HOUSE OF LORDS. Pamphlet. Price 6d. nett.

EDWARD CARPENTER: THE MAN AND HIS MESSAGE. Pamphlet by TOM SWAN, with two portraits and copious extracts from the above works. Price 6d. nett.

Now Ready

Robert Owen: Pioneer of Social Reform.
By Joseph Clayton. 6d. nett. Quarter cloth, gilt top, 1s. nett. Postages, 1d. and 2d.

Henry George and His Gospel. By Lieut.-Col. D. C. Pedder. 6d. nett and 1s. nett. Postages, 1d. and 2d.

Vols. 1 and 2 of The Social Reformers Series.

"A new and promising series likely to prove at once successful and timely."—*Leicester Post*. "The writers have recognised the profound importance of their subjects, and each has produced a comprehensive, lucid, and fascinating book."—*Dundee Advertiser*. "One of the best little books I have come across on Robert Owen."—*Yorkshire Factory Times*. "So many recruits are daily coming into the Socialist forces that a series of this character is extremely timely."—*Pioneer*. "Promises to be of special value to all who are interested in the progressive movements of the day."—*Aberdeen Free Press*.

Gems from Henry George. 112 pages.
Post free, 7d.

"Not many people now care to face a reading of all Henry George's volumes, but there should be a wide public for this collection of selected passages from his published works. They give in tabloid form the best of the great social reformer."—*Dundee Advertiser*.

The Sanity of William Blake. By Greville MacDonald, M.D. Six Illustrations. Grey boards. Post free, 1s. 2d.

"An altogether admirable little essay."—*Daily Chronicle*. "A masterly study of an extraordinary genius."—*Newcastle Chronicle*. "The illustrations alone are almost worth the price asked for the booklet."—*Glasgow Herald*.

The Commonsense of Municipal Trading.
By G. Bernard Shaw. 6d. nett. Postage, 1½d. Quarter cloth, gilt top. Post free, 1s. 2d.

A new and popular edition of this admirable and convincing work, with a new eight-page preface.

The Great Companions. By Henry Bryan Binns. Boards, 2s. nett. Postage, 3d.

"A vivid and glowing book."—*Observer*. "There is life and passion in this little book."—*Inquirer*. "I see in Mr. Binns one of the pioneers of the new purpose."—*New Age*. "He is not so large and boisterous as Whitman, but more delicate, more perceptive."—*Nation*. "He has something to say, and he says it freshly and individually."—*Morning Leader*.

London: A. C. Fifield, 44 Fleet Street, E.C.

New Books

Spiritual Perfection. A Discussion. By Thomas Clune. Fscap. 8vo, grey boards, 1s. nett. Post-free, 1s. 1½d.

"A thoughtful dialogue."—*The Times*. "A readable and acutely reasoned philosophical dialogue, discussing in a suggestive and interesting way the formation of character upon a basis of Christianity."—*Scotsman*. "A thoughtful contribution to a great subject."—*Scottish Review*.

Count Louis, and other Poems. By Henry H. Schloesser, author of "The Fallen Temple." Fscap. 8vo, grey boards, 1s. nett. Post-free, 1s. 1½d.

Socialism: A Solution and Safeguard. Open Letters to Mr. J. St. Loe Strachey, in reply to "Problems and Perils of Socialism." By Charles Derwent Smith. 6d. nett. Postage, 1d.

British Aristocracy and the House of Lords. By Edward Carpenter. 6d. nett. Postage, 1d.

An enquiry, a forecast, and a suggestion.

William Morris: Craftsman—Socialist. By Holbrook Jackson, author of "Bernard Shaw: A Monograph." Social Reformers Series, No. 3. 6d. nett. Postage, 1d. Quarter cloth, 1s. nett. Postage, 2d.

Nature Poems and Others. By William H. Davies, author of "The Soul's Destroyer," "Autobiography of a Super-Tramp," etc. Fscap. 8vo, grey boards, 1s. nett. Post-free, 1s. 1½d.

The publisher believes this new volume of Poems will delight the readers of Mr. Davies' previous work, and add greatly to the author's reputation.

How are the Clergy Paid? A Popular History of the Tithe Laws. By T. Bennett, LL.D., B.A.(Lond.) 6d. nett. Postage, 1d.

Disestablishment: What it Means. By T. Bennett, LL.D., B.A.(Lond.). A sane and reasonable examination. 6d. net. Postage, 1d.

London: A. C. Fifield, 44 Fleet Street, E.C.

Trieste

Trieste Publishing has a massive catalogue of classic book titles. Our aim is to provide readers with the highest quality reproductions of fiction and non-fiction literature that has stood the test of time. The many thousands of books in our collection have been sourced from libraries and private collections around the world.

The titles that Trieste Publishing has chosen to be part of the collection have been scanned to simulate the original. Our readers see the books the same way that their first readers did decades or a hundred or more years ago. Books from that period are often spoiled by imperfections that did not exist in the original. Imperfections could be in the form of blurred text, photographs, or missing pages. It is highly unlikely that this would occur with one of our books. Our extensive quality control ensures that the readers of Trieste Publishing's books will be delighted with their purchase. Our staff has thoroughly reviewed every page of all the books in the collection, repairing, or if necessary, rejecting titles that are not of the highest quality. This process ensures that the reader of one of Trieste Publishing's titles receives a volume that faithfully reproduces the original, and to the maximum degree possible, gives them the experience of owning the original work.

We pride ourselves on not only creating a pathway to an extensive reservoir of books of the finest quality, but also providing value to every one of our readers. Generally, Trieste books are purchased singly - on demand, however they may also be purchased in bulk. Readers interested in bulk purchases are invited to contact us directly to enquire about our tailored bulk rates. Email: customerservice@triestepublishing.com

You May Also Like

Rochester ways

Charles Mulford Robinson

ISBN: 9780649078530
Paperback: 80 pages
Dimensions: 6.14 x 0.17 x 9.21 inches
Language: eng

The Link, Vol. 30, No. 4, April 1972

Edward I. Swanson

ISBN: 9780649077304
Paperback: 80 pages
Dimensions: 6.14 x 0.17 x 9.21 inches
Language: eng

www.triestepublishing.com

You May Also Like

The open way into the book of Revelation. God's sevenfold way to consummations or fulfillments of prophecies

M. M. Eshelman

ISBN: 9780649376476
Paperback: 232 pages
Dimensions: 6.14 x 0.49 x 9.21 inches
Language: eng

Clarendon Press Series. Easy Passages for Translation into Latin

John Young Sargent

ISBN: 9781760579708
Paperback: 176 pages
Dimensions: 6.0 x 0.38 x 9.0 inches
Language: eng

www.triestepublishing.com

You May Also Like

Shut Your Mouth and Save Your Life

George Catlin

ISBN: 9781760570491
Paperback: 118 pages
Dimensions: 6.14 x 0.25 x 9.21 inches
Language: eng

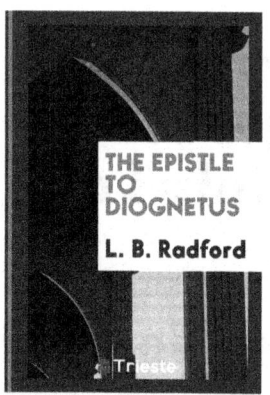

The Epistle to Diognetus

L. B. Radford

ISBN: 9781760570934
Paperback: 106 pages
Dimensions: 6.14 x 0.22 x 9.21 inches
Language: eng

www.triestepublishing.com

You May Also Like

Bulgarian horrors and the question of the East

W. E. Gladstone

ISBN: 9781760571146
Paperback: 46 pages
Dimensions: 6.14 x 0.09 x 9.21 inches
Language: eng

Snow-bound: A Winter Idyl

John Greenleaf Whittier

ISBN: 9781760571528
Paperback: 64 pages
Dimensions: 5.5 x 0.13 x 8.25 inches
Language: eng

Find more of our titles on our website. We have a selection of thousands of titles that will interest you. Please visit

www.triestepublishing.com